THE [illegible]D IN OUR HEARTS

Key for Healing and Revival for Our Generation

COMFORT EKUNDAYO

Author services by: www.OpulentBooks.net

ISBN: 978-1-916691-83-4

Dedication

I dedicate this book to my parents and my dear grandma, who raised me to trust the Lord from a very young age. My life will never be the same because of the foundation they laid, the prayers they prayed, and the example they showed. Their unwavering faith and godly walk have been a light that continues to guide my path.

Acknowledgements

First and foremost, I give all glory and thanks to God, the giver of life, wisdom, and purpose. Without His grace, this book would not have come into being.

I honour my spiritual mentors who have poured into my life and ministry over the years. To Rev. Morris Cerullo, whose teachings deeply impacted my understanding of kingdom leadership, and to Pastor Sunday Adelaja, whose guidance and wisdom helped shape my ministry and strengthened my leadership calling.

I also acknowledge the role Kensington Temple

played in my development. My time there taught me invaluable lessons on cell group leadership, spiritual growth, and the power of community.

My heartfelt thanks to Joe Benjamin, my book coach and publisher, for his encouragement, guidance, and support throughout this journey. His input and that of his team have been vital to the completion of this work.

Finally, I am grateful for all those, named and unnamed, who have touched my life, directly or indirectly. This book stands as a testimony to the truth I have known and practised, for as the Bible says, "You shall know the truth, and the truth shall make you free."

Thank you all.

Table of Contents

CHAPTER 1

The Love of God

The message of this book is simple yet profound. Everything begins and ends with love. Not just any love, but the love of God. The love that created the universe, redeemed mankind, and sustains the Church today. Without this love, nothing in the Christian life can stand. It is not a side issue or an optional virtue. The love of God is the very foundation of Christian living.

We see this foundation laid from the very beginning of the Bible. In Genesis, God created man in His own image, not out of duty but out of desire for relationship. He formed Adam and gave him a companion, Eve, so he would not be alone. From the start, God designed humanity for love, connection, and fellowship. Love was present before the fall, before sin entered the world. It was part of God's original intention.

When the Lord gave the commandments to His people, love was central. *"You shall love the Lord your God with all your heart, with all your soul, and with all your strength"* (Deuteronomy 6:5). This commandment remains the greatest of all, echoed by Jesus Himself in the Gospels. Love for God is not partial; it requires all of who we are. But it does not end there. We are also commanded to love our neighbour as ourselves (Leviticus 19:18).

Jesus lived out this love during His earthly ministry. His time on earth may have been just over three years, but He demonstrated more love in that short time than many do in a lifetime. He loved the broken, the rejected, the sick, and the sinful. He healed not just to prove His power, but because He was moved with compassion. Every act of mercy was an act of love. Every miracle was born from the heart of God.

Jesus did not hoard His power. He told His disciples, "*Most assuredly, I say to you, he who believes in Me, the works that I do he will do also; and greater works than these he will do, because I go to My Father*" (John 14:12). That is love. He wanted others to do more, go further, rise higher. Love does not compete; it empowers.

When love is truly present in the heart, it changes everything. The kind of love the Bible speaks of is not shallow or sentimental. It is a love rooted in sacrifice, sustained by grace, and revealed through action. It is not always about liking someone's personality or choices. Love is deeper than preference. It is spiritual and divine.

Many confuse love with liking. Liking is based on what appeals to us. Love is a choice that reflects God's heart, even when it is uncomfortable. "*Though I speak with the tongues of men and of angels, but have not love, I have become sounding brass or a clanging cymbal*" (1 Corinthians 13:1). The Apostle Paul reminds us that without love, all gifts and efforts are meaningless.

Love in ministry is not optional; it is essential. If a pastor or leader ministers without love, they will eventually fall into pride, comparison, and manipulation. Today, we see ministers who perform miracles and preach powerfully, yet their hearts are full of envy and bitterness. This is a dangerous deception. Without love, even the most visible ministry is hollow.

The Church must return to love. Not love as an idea, but love as a lifestyle. We must pray, "Lord, fill my heart with Your love. Give me a revelation of Your love." When we are filled with God's love, we cannot hate, we cannot slander, we cannot rejoice when others fall. Instead, we will pray for our enemies, bless those who curse us, and intercede for the restoration of others.

Jesus washed the feet of His disciples, knowing that one of them would betray Him. He told them, *"For I have given you an example, that you should do as I have done to you"* (John 13:15). This is servant-hearted love. This is the model of ministry we are called to follow.

Love does not make us weak. It makes us like Christ. And when we are like Christ, we become agents of healing and revival in a broken world.

If you truly love God, you will love His people. You will not seek to tear others down but to lift them up. You will not hoard your anointing, but you will pour it out. You will pray not only for your own success but for the advancement of the whole Body of Christ.

The Church is in need of healing, and love is the medicine. Revival will not come through noise or numbers, but through hearts transformed by the love of God. Let us return to that love. Let us live it, preach it, and become vessels of it. Because the greatest of these is love.

Reflect and Respond

In what ways have you personally experienced the love of God in your life, and how has it shaped your relationship with others?

Are there areas in your heart or ministry where love has grown cold or been replaced by performance, pride, or comparison?

What would it look like for you to live out love as a lifestyle; especially towards those who are difficult to love?

CHAPTER 2

Love in Action

Love is not proven in words, it is revealed in action. The Church is called to be the expression of Christ on the earth, but too often, the way we treat one another reflects anything but His love. Many believers have walked into churches filled with hope, only to walk out broken, rejected, and wounded. This ought not to be so.

My own awakening to this reality came in the 1980s. Until then, I had assumed pastors loved one another. I grew up in a home filled with love, with godly parents who never condemned others. My surroundings taught me compassion and unity. So when I first encountered jealousy, betrayal, and hatred among senior church leaders, it shook me to my core.

I remember a particular incident that left a mark on my life. A well-known Nigerian pastor had come to London to start a ministry. On the surface, he was welcomed by other leaders: smiles, handshakes, words of support. But behind the scenes, some of those same leaders visited the man who had offered this pastor a meeting venue and pressured him to revoke the offer. They wanted him out.

The man who had offered his space refused. He said, "If I chase this man away now, you are the ones who should rebuke me. You are our elders. You should uphold love, not division." That day, I was so disturbed that I took the wrong train. I was not asleep, but the emotional shock of what I had witnessed made me lose awareness of my surroundings. That memory still lives with me.

Years later, many of those elders have passed, but I still wonder, where did they end up? After all their preaching, healing, and signs, did they carry unforgiveness and envy to the grave? More troubling is what I have observed since. The next generation of leaders have become worse. The legacy passed down was not one of love, but of rivalry.

Jesus warned us, "*By this all will know that you are My disciples, if you have love for one another*" (John 13:35). Love is not a simple sermon; it is a sign. When the Church lacks love, we lose credibility with the world.

Today, we hear of churches praying against other churches. Leaders rejoicing when others fall.

Entire ministries built on tearing others down. This is not the Gospel. If the enemy has managed to turn our pulpits into platforms of competition, then we have strayed far from the cross. True love does not envy. It rejoices in the success of others. It covers, it heals, it builds.

Even when correction is necessary, it should come from a place of love, not vengeance. Galatians 6:1 says, *"Brethren, if a man is overtaken in any trespass, you who are spiritual restore such a one in a spirit of gentleness, considering yourself lest you also be tempted"*.

Love in action means standing with the weak, not exploiting them. It means lifting the fallen, not gossiping about them. It means protecting the vulnerable, not abusing them. And yes, it means praying for other ministries, not plotting their downfall.

There can be no revival without a return to love. Our anointing means nothing without compassion. Our sermons are noise without kindness. Our churches are hollow without grace.

The love of God must be our motive, our method, and our message. If the Church is to be a hospital for the hurting, we must stop inflicting wounds and start offering healing. Let our love be more than a greeting at the door. Let it be seen in how we treat the least, the lost, and even those we do not understand. The world is watching, and more importantly, so is God.

Reflect and Respond

How has your view of love changed after seeing how it must be expressed through action rather than words?

In your church or community, who are the overlooked or hurting individuals you feel called to serve or notice more intentionally?

What does “love in action” look like in your day-to-day interactions, especially in how you respond to injustice or rivalry?

CHAPTER 3

Rebuilding Trust in the Church

"A new commandment I give to you, that you love one another; as I have loved you, that you also love one another. By this all will know that you are My disciples, if you have love for one another."

(John 13:34–35)

The words of Jesus Christ are crystal clear. Love is not a suggestion—it is a command. It is the very foundation upon which trust, fellowship, and unity in the Church must be built. Yet, as I sat before the Lord, He began to deal with my heart about a painful truth: the Church has, in many ways, failed to walk in this love.

There is disunity. There is criticism. There is envy. And these things grieve the heart of God.

I saw in the Spirit a people who were meant to labour together in God's vineyard, but instead were tearing down one another's work. One pastor criticising another pastor for focusing on healing. One leader mocking deliverance ministries. Some belittling others who are called to teach prosperity and Biblical wealth.

Why? Because they do not understand. And rather than seeking God about it, they lash out in judgement.

If you do not understand another person's calling, the mature thing is to seek God in prayer.

Ask the Father for wisdom. Ask Him to reveal whether their work is of Him. We must stop doing the enemy's work for him. "*Do not speak evil of one another, brethren. He who speaks evil of a brother and judges his brother, speaks evil of the law and judges the law.*" (James 4:11)

We are not judges over another man's servant. If someone says they are called by God and are ministering in a way different from yours, pray for them. If it is not of God, the Lord Himself will correct it. But if it is of God, you are fighting against His purpose.

I have witnessed with great sorrow people who go to the mountains to pray, not to intercede for the lost or seek revival, but to pray *against* other ministers. To curse what they do not understand. This is not the way of Christ. This is not the Spirit of the Lord.

No one can pull down what God Himself has built. When something is born of the Spirit, it is indestructible. The weapons formed against it may rise, but they shall not prosper. *"Every plant which My heavenly Father has not planted will be uprooted."* (Matthew 15:13) The reverse is also true: what God *has* planted will stand.

Many ministers unknowingly curse themselves by opposing others in the name of discernment. They hinder their own progress and wonder why their ministries do not grow. They do not realise they are blocking their own blessing.

We must repent.

We must return to the simplicity of love. The Lord is calling His Bride back to His heart. He is not impressed by titles, buildings, or platforms. He is moved by hearts that mirror His own—hearts that love deeply and serve selflessly.

Let me be honest. I have seen a pastor serving faithfully in a ministry, only for another leader, one who was supposed to be like a spiritual father, to go behind his back and sabotage him. They went to the person who had given him a room to live and minister, and they convinced him to evict him. All in the name of "protecting the church". This is not God. This is manipulation. This is control. And it causes deep wounds in the body of Christ.

Such actions create distrust. When believers are hurt by leaders, it takes time to rebuild their confidence. It takes humility, authenticity, and a genuine desire to reflect Christ. If we truly love God, we will love one another. We will pray for one another. We will build each other up and not tear each other down.

This is what scripture says: *"Let nothing be done through selfish ambition or conceit, but in lowliness of mind let each esteem others better than himself.*" (Philippians 2:3)

This is not just about being kind; this is about survival. The Church cannot endure the pressures of this generation if we continue to cannibalise our own.

A house divided against itself cannot stand. We must be healed from the inside. And healing begins with love. I urge every leader, every minister, every believer to check your heart. Are you tearing others down in the name of zeal? Are you misusing your mouth to curse rather than to bless? Are you resisting what God is doing simply because it does not look like your own ministry?

Repent.

God is not mocked. He sees every motive. He hears every whisper. But He also offers healing. He offers reconciliation. He offers a fresh start. Let love rebuild the Church. Let love restore what envy has broken. Let love heal what pride has wounded. Let us love as Christ has loved us. Then, and only then, will the world know that we are truly His disciples.

Reflect and Respond

Have you ever criticised a ministry or leader you didn't understand? What could maturity have looked like in that moment?

In what ways can you help rebuild trust within your church community?

How can you honour other people's callings, even when they don't align with your own preferences or traditions?

CHAPTER 4

When Leadership Hurts

I remember a time when I witnessed something in the Church that truly devastated me. A pastor who was faithfully serving in a ministry was told to leave the house where the Church was being hosted. The very man he regarded as a spiritual father went behind his back to the landlord and asked for him to be evicted. I was there that day. Somehow, God had placed me in the room when they came to deliver that blow. They had already planned it. They came, they spoke to the landlord, and tried to remove him. But thank God the landlord was a man of God and didn't go along with their wickedness.

I left that place shaken. I couldn't believe what I had just seen. These were leaders, elders, people we look up to in the faith. And yet their actions were full of envy, sabotage, and betrayal. I missed my train home that day. The shock was too much. It made me think deeply about the condition of the Church and the pain we inflict on one another, especially when it's done in the name of leadership.

When leadership hurts, it cuts deep. The Church is supposed to be a place of refuge, restoration and spiritual family. But too often, it becomes a place of rejection, jealousy, and judgment. Jesus did not model that kind of leadership. He knew Judas would betray Him, but He still washed his feet. He knew Peter would deny Him, yet He restored him. He never retaliated. He never sent anyone away out of pride or politics. He led with love.

1 Peter 5:2–3 says "*Shepherd the flock of God which is among you, serving as overseers, not by compulsion but willingly, not for dishonest gain but eagerly; nor as being lords over those entrusted to you, but being examples to the flock.*"

If we truly claim to be His disciples, our leadership must be defined by love. Not competition, manipulation or power plays. As 1 Peter 5:2–3 reminds us, we are called to shepherd with humility and serve as examples to the flock—not as controllers or abusers of power. We must be willing to examine our hearts. Have I become bitter because of Church hurt? Have I started projecting my wounds onto others? Or worse, have I become the one who hurts others in the name of ministry?

There was a time I experienced deep pain at the hands of someone I once called a leader. It was not just a leader, but someone who had embraced me like family. We would sit together, laugh together, and I truly believed we were building something genuine for the Kingdom of God. In fact, they often referred to me as a "daughter." That word—"daughter"—meant something to me. It spoke of trust, safety, and belonging. So when betrayal came from that same person, the wound cut far deeper than I could ever have imagined.

I remember the moment the mask fell off. The way they turned on me, suddenly and without warning. It was as though I had become an enemy overnight. The same person who had embraced me with open arms began to shut doors in my face. And the worst part? It wasn't just personal—it became public. It became a matter of ministry, of influence, and of reputation. And all I could think was, "How could someone who speaks of God's love, who preaches on Sundays, turn so cold and calculated in private?"

That experience made me question everything. For a while, I stopped trusting church leaders. I would walk into a building and feel guarded, constantly watching my back, afraid to get too close. I began to see that many people were operating from a place of performance, not genuine love. The pulpit became a stage for pride, not a platform for service. And the sheep—God's precious people—were left bleeding while the shepherds polished their images.

I am not writing this to stir division, but to tell the truth. Many people reading this have experienced Church hurt. Some have been lied to, manipulated, overlooked, or even abused by those who were meant to guide them. Some have given their last pound to support a vision, only to be cast aside when they were no longer useful. Others have served faithfully, only to be pushed out by politics and pride. And still, they carry the pain quietly, afraid to speak, afraid to be judged. But I want to say this: God sees.

Psalm 147:3 says, "*He heals the brokenhearted and binds up their wounds.*" That includes the wounds inflicted by religious leaders. Jesus Himself was betrayed by one of His own disciples. He knows what it is to be sold out by someone close. So when we bring Him our pain, He does not dismiss it. He understands it.

Over time, I had to learn how to heal. Healing did not mean going back to pretend nothing happened. It meant acknowledging the pain, forgiving, and releasing it into God's hands. I had to ask God to restore my heart so that bitterness would not take root. I had to choose love again, even when it felt like a risk.

If you have been hurt by leadership, I want you to know that your pain is valid, but it does not have to define your future. The love of God is not limited to a man or a ministry. His love is pure, healing, and trustworthy. Ask Him to heal you. Ask Him to help you trust again. And most of all, allow Him to remind you of who He is, not based on how people have treated you, but based on His unchanging character.

Isaiah 61:1 says, *"The Spirit of the Lord God is upon Me, because the Lord has anointed Me to preach good tidings to the poor; He has sent Me to heal the brokenhearted."* That includes you.

When leadership hurts, Jesus heals. There is healing in the presence of God. I had to bring those wounds before the Lord. I had to cry, to forgive, and to ask Him to cleanse me from any bitterness that was starting to take root. And I encourage you to do the same. If you've been hurt by leadership, don't carry that pain alone. Bring it before the Lord. He sees. He knows. And He will restore you.

If you are in leadership, take this as a warning and a call to humility. We are not called to control people, but to serve them. We are not above the flock—we are among them. And if you've made mistakes, repent. Let God refine your heart and teach you how to lead with compassion.

God is building a pure Bride. And in that Bride, there is no room for ego, control, or envy. May our leadership reflect the love of Christ, even when it hurts. May we heal from our wounds and not pass them on. May we learn from our mistakes and walk in the Spirit, not the flesh. Lord, help us lead like You. Amen.

Reflect and Respond

Have you ever experienced hurt at the hands of a spiritual leader? How has that experience affected your view of God, leadership, or the Church?

____

____

____

What steps can you take today to begin healing from past wounds so they don't shape how you lead or relate to others?

____

____

____

____

If you are in leadership, how can you ensure that you serve from a place of love, humility, and healing rather than from pain or pride?

CHAPTER 5

Obedience

Love is not merely an emotion; it is demonstrated through action, and at the heart of that action is obedience. Jesus said, "*If you love Me, keep My commandments*" (John 14:15). Obedience is the visible fruit of our invisible love for God. In the context of the Church, where division, pride, and personal ambition often quench the Spirit, it is obedience to God's Word that realigns us with heaven's heart. Revival cannot come where rebellion remains. Healing cannot flow where disobedience hinders. This chapter invites us to rediscover the joy and power of obeying God, not out of fear or duty, but out of deep love for the One who gave everything for us. When we obey, we partner with God's purposes and position ourselves for His presence. Obedience is one of the least glamorous but most powerful principles in the Kingdom of God. Many believers crave the fulfilment of divine promises or long to walk in supernatural power, yet they resist the very bridge that carries them from desire to manifestation: obedience. God does not bless ambition; He blesses alignment.

When God gives us an instruction, it is not merely a suggestion or a guideline. It is a test of the heart. Obedience is the currency of covenant. From the days of Abraham to the teachings of Christ, Scripture makes it clear that obedience is better than sacrifice (1 Samuel 15:22). You can fast, tithe, sing, and serve, but if you are not obedient to the Lord's voice, you have disconnected yourself from the true channel of divine favour.

Jesus himself modelled perfect obedience. In John 5:19, He said, "*Most assuredly, I say to you, the Son can do nothing of Himself, but what He sees the Father do; for whatever He does, the Son also does in like manner.*" Christ's miracles flowed from His submission, not from His ambition.

Too many people want a new thing from God while clinging to old instructions. They cry out for power but refuse to obey the process. They desire elevation but ignore correction. And yet the path to spiritual breakthrough is not paved with emotion or opinion, but obedience.

I remember speaking to a young believer who had been fasting and praying for divine direction. For weeks, she received no response. Then, one day, she said, "God told me to forgive someone months ago, and I never did." That moment of realisation unlocked the flow of divine communication. Obedience had been the missing key.

When God gives you a word, your response determines your reward. Delay in obedience is still disobedience. Every instruction from God carries within it the seed of blessing. But that seed only bears fruit when it is acted upon.

James 1:22 reminds us, *"But be doers of the word, and not hearers only, deceiving yourselves."* Many deceive themselves into thinking that understanding Scripture is the same as living it. But true transformation begins at the point of applied obedience.

In this season, God is not looking for the loudest voice or the most gifted hand. He is looking for obedient hearts. People who will say like Mary, "*Behold the maidservant of the Lord! Let it be to me according to your word*" (Luke 1:38). That single act of obedience changed the history of the world.

Have you delayed an instruction from God? Is there something He told you to do—serve, forgive, give, go, speak—that you have shelved in fear or rebellion? Remember, your obedience might be the answer to someone else's prayer.

Just as Peter obeyed the voice of Jesus to cast the net one more time, even after toiling all night (Luke 5:4–6), your next miracle may hinge on your next obedient step. The fish were not in the sea randomly—they were waiting on the other side of obedience.

Let us return to that place where we tremble at God's word, where we delight in His commands, and where obedience is not a burden but a joy. For in that place, we will walk in power, inherit promise, and please the heart of our Father. May we never forget: obedience is not just for our benefit. It is for the glory of God, the fulfilment of purpose, and the advancement of His Kingdom on earth.

Reflect and Respond

Is there a specific instruction from God that you've delayed or avoided? What's holding you back from obeying it fully?

How do you respond when God's instructions challenge your comfort, routine, or personal ambition?

In what ways can you cultivate a lifestyle where obedience becomes your first response, not your last resort?

CHAPTER 6

God's Love Versus Religion

Jesus never came to establish a religion. He came to reveal the Father's heart and reconcile us back to Him through love. That love is the foundation of everything. Without it, our preaching, our singing, our praying, and our ministry become nothing but noise. As the Apostle Paul reminds us in 1 Corinthians 13:1–2, even the most powerful spiritual gifts mean nothing without love.

1 Corinthians 13:1–2 states: *"Though I speak with the tongues of men and of angels, but have not love, I*

have become sounding brass or a clanging cymbal. And though I have the gift of prophecy, and understand all mysteries and all knowledge... but have not love, I am nothing."

This love is not about mere words or outward appearance. It is not about wearing a title or being recognised as a minister. It is not about how big your Church is, how many events you run, or how many scriptures you can recite. True love is what sustains us. True love is what gives meaning to everything we do. Without the love of God flowing through us, we cannot endure the journey. We will fall into performance, jealousy, pride, and strife. That is the trap of religion.

Religion tells you to do things to be accepted. Love tells you that you are accepted; therefore, you serve. Religion performs. Love obeys. Religion competes. Love completes. Religion is based on rules. Love is led by the Spirit. Many people are preaching, prophesying, and even pastoring today, but there is no love in their hearts. And because of that, their ministry feels dry. Their efforts feel heavy. Their walk feels burdensome. It is not that God has abandoned them. It is that they have not allowed His love to fully flow through them.

As I reflected on this, I was reminded of how many ministers are doing good works outwardly but are spiritually empty within. The truth is, you cannot truly love God and hate your brother. You cannot say you serve God while tearing down His children. You cannot claim to walk in the Spirit while harbouring envy and bitterness. This is why the Bible tells us to examine ourselves. In 2 Corinthians 13:5, it says, "*Examine yourselves as to whether you are in the faith. Test yourselves. Do you not know yourselves, that Jesus Christ is in you?—unless indeed you are disqualified."*

This call is not just for pastors or preachers. It is for every believer. We are called to be a reflection of Christ. That means we must lay down performance and take up intimacy. We must lay down appearance and pick up substance. We must let go of religion and embrace relationship.

I have learned that you can be doing everything right externally, but still be disconnected from God internally. You can be so busy doing ministry that you forget to minister to the Lord. You can be so preoccupied with building your platform that you forget to build your relationship with God. I have been there. I have known what it feels like to go through the motions, yet feel empty inside.

But I also know what it feels like when His love fills you afresh, when His presence becomes real again. When the Word comes alive and prayer flows from your spirit instead of from duty. That is the difference. Love fuels true ministry. Love restores your soul. Love keeps your heart soft and your spirit aligned.

So this chapter is a call to return—to return to your first love, to return to the simplicity of the gospel, to return to the presence of God. Let us not build ministries that impress people but leave us dry. Let us build altars where God's fire can fall. Let us live and lead from a place of love, not religion. And let us remember, love is the evidence. Love is the fruit. Love is the mark of a true disciple. Let everything we do be done in love. For only love will remain.

Reflect and Respond

In your walk with God, are there areas where performance or routine has replaced true intimacy with Him?

How can you shift from doing ministry for approval or image to serving from a place of love and relationship?

What practical steps can you take to ensure your faith is rooted in love, not religion?

CHAPTER 7

Becoming True Fishers of Men

When Jesus called His first disciples, He did not call them to fame, title or comfort. He called them to follow Him and become fishers of men. In Matthew 4:19, He said to Peter and Andrew, *"Follow Me, and I will make you fishers of men."* That call still stands today. It is not just for pastors or evangelists. It is for every believer.

We are not here merely to attend church services or join religious programmes. We are here to carry the light of Christ and win souls for the Kingdom. That is our true assignment. And if we are not doing that, we must ask ourselves, why?

I have watched over the years how many in the Church have lost their focus. We have become busy with positions, titles, fundraising, and maintaining buildings. We have exchanged the simplicity of the gospel for the complexity of church structure. But Jesus never told us to build empires. He told us to make disciples.

So I ask you today, are you truly fishing for souls, or have you been caught up in the business of Church?

Many of us think our job is done when we invite someone to Church. But that is not enough. We must lead them to Christ. We must teach them the Word. We must walk with them until they are strong in faith. That is what discipleship looks like.

That is what it means to be a fisher of men.

When Peter and John healed the man at the gate in Acts 3, they were not performing a show. They were carrying the power of God. The Bible says, *"Then Peter said, 'Silver and gold I do not have, but what I do have I give you: In the name of Jesus Christ of Nazareth, rise up and walk'"* (Acts 3:6). That power came because they had been with Jesus. They had learned to love, serve, and obey.

You cannot become a true fisher of men without the love of God in your heart. You must love people enough to pray for them, to walk with them, to correct them in love, and to point them to Christ. You cannot win souls while harbouring bitterness or jealousy. You cannot carry the anointing of God while comparing yourself to others. The harvest requires a clean heart, a humble spirit, and a willingness to be used by God.

So many people in the body of Christ are busy with ministry, but they are not touching lives. They are not soul winners. They are titleholders. But God is not impressed by our titles. He is looking for fruit. He is looking for labourers.

In John 15:16, Jesus says, "*You did not choose Me, but I chose you and appointed you that you should go and bear fruit, and that your fruit should remain.*" Soul-winning is not optional. It is our appointment. It is our assignment. It is our joy.

And it is not about filling seats in our churches. Whether the soul ends up in your Church or another one, it does not matter. What matters is that they come to know Jesus. This is not a competition. This is Kingdom work.

If someone in your Church begins to grow and walk in their calling, do not see them as a threat. Support them. Encourage them. Let them rise. You are not the owner of the Church. Jesus is. If your role is to plant, then plant. If your role is to water, then water. But know this: it is God who gives the increase (1 Corinthians 3:6–7).

Becoming a fisher of men also means understanding your purpose. You are not here by accident. God has placed people around you who need the light you carry. Your story, your testimony, your love, these are tools in God's hands. Use them.

Jesus is still calling today. He is calling you and me to lay aside distractions and follow Him. To love people. To serve with sincerity. To preach the gospel not just with words, but with our lives.

Let these words stir your heart. Let it remind you of why you were saved. You were saved to serve. You were delivered to deliver others. You were found so that you could help others be found. Lord, make me a fisher of men. Teach me to walk in love. Let my life point people to You.

A Reflection on Soul-Winning and the Heart of Discipleship

Before we go out to win souls, we must ask ourselves a hard question: Are we doing it out of love for Jesus and for the people we want to reach, or are we doing it for selfish reasons? Is it to grow our Church, to be seen, or to fill empty seats? Or is it truly because we want people to know Christ, experience salvation, and spend eternity with Him?

I have gone out many times to evangelise. I have knocked on doors in my neighbourhood, even when I did not belong to a church at the time. I just wanted people to hear the Word of God. It was not about building a ministry. It was not about numbers. It was simply because I had something in my heart that I wanted others to know.

Jesus said, "*Go therefore and make disciples of all the nations...*" (Matthew 28:19). He did not say, "Go and fill your church." Winning souls is important, but making disciples is the real command. We must consider: where are the people we bring in going to be discipled? Who is going to walk with them, teach them, and help them grow in Christ?

One sister once asked, "Where are all the souls that were brought in during evangelism?" At the time, I did not understand what she meant. But now I do. Winning souls is only the beginning. If we truly love the people we bring to Christ, we will have a plan to walk with them and help them mature.

I have seen many new believers, especially those from non-Christian backgrounds like Muslims or Hindus, come to Church only to leave shortly after.

Often, they feel out of place or overlooked. No one befriends them. Everyone is caught up in their own world. This should not be so. "*Let brotherly love continue*" (Hebrews 13:1). Love looks out for the stranger. Love creates space at the table.

In some churches, I have seen the same groups of people gather for years, often only connecting with those from their own background or culture. But the love of God does not separate us by nationality or familiarity. It unites us in Christ. "*There is neither Jew nor Greek, there is neither slave nor free... for you are all one in Christ Jesus*" (Galatians 3:28).

We need to be intentional about creating a church culture where new people feel safe and seen. Discipleship is not just a six-week class. It is a lifelong journey. We need people who will walk with new believers until they, too, can disciple others. Paul told Timothy, *"The things that you have heard from me... commit these to faithful men who will be able to teach others also"* (2 Timothy 2:2).

In my years of leading a small group, I have seen how people behave when they feel familiar. Many stay within their comfort zone. But if we are going to win the world, we must move beyond what is familiar and embrace the Kingdom culture of love, honour, and inclusion.

The Church must take another step forward. Not just institutionally, but individually. If every believer looked after one soul with the love of Christ, the Kingdom of God would multiply in ways we cannot imagine. Sometimes, I pray and say, "Lord, You have to do something in me. Let Your love fill me so deeply that I see every person—saved or unsaved—as someone worth pursuing."

The call to win souls must flow from the heart

of God. It must be more than handing out tracts or inviting someone to Church. It must involve relationship, follow-up, and discipleship. "*By this all will know that you are My disciples, if you have love for one another*" (John 13:35).

Let us not win souls to satisfy statistics or to impress others. Let us win them because Christ first loved us. Let us love them enough to walk with them, to disciple them, and to see them grow until they, too, become soul-winners. That is the heart of the Gospel.

May the love of God move us beyond culture, comfort, and convenience. May it compel us to reach out, embrace, and disciple with compassion and purpose. Amen.

Reflect and Respond

Are you actively sharing the message of Jesus and discipling others, or have you become distracted by titles, roles, or routine church activity?

____

____

____

What barriers—such as fear, comfort, or cultural familiarity—might be holding you back from reaching those who need the Gospel?

____

____

____

____

How can you create space in your life or church community to walk with new believers until they grow and disciple others?

CHAPTER 8

Healing The Church

The Church is in desperate need of healing, not only from external attacks, but from internal wounds. Manipulation, pride, jealousy, and control have found a place in the hearts of many leaders. This is not the Church Jesus died for. This is not the Body He calls His own. Where there should be shepherds, there are predators. Where there should be humility, there is hierarchy. The love of God has been replaced with the love of power.

True ministry cannot survive on control. Many so-called leaders today have turned pulpits into stages for performance and platforms for personal gain. Love has been lost in the race for numbers, prestige, and wealth. We see ministers who publicly preach power, yet privately abuse those closest to them. The contradiction is staggering.

Recently, I witnessed a situation that broke my heart. A well-known pastor, travelling between America, Canada, and Nigeria, was being confronted because his wife's family had not seen her or their children in four years. This woman's family cried out publicly, begging to know if their daughter was even alive. The man ignored them, even though they only asked for confirmation of her well-being. How can such a person continue to minister as though nothing is wrong?

The Bible says, "*He who does not love does not know*

God, for God is love" (1 John 4:8). If you deny your own family compassion, what gospel are you preaching? If your ministry causes harm to your own household, what example are you setting for your congregation? If you are called to shepherd God's people, how can you mistreat those in your own home?

The Church is sick, and much of it stems from the leadership. We have replaced the servant-hearted model of Jesus with a throne-like mentality. Jesus said, "*You know that those who are considered rulers over the Gentiles lord it over them... Yet it shall not be so among you; but whoever desires to become great among you shall be your servant*" (Mark 10:42-43).

Instead, many are praying against other churches, manipulating members, and competing for influence. This is not revival. It is rebellion. It is a sign that the Spirit of God is being grieved.

We have made idols of influence. Some leaders hoard spiritual gifts and envy those who operate in similar grace. They isolate, they accuse, they try to destroy others behind the scenes, even praying against them. This is witchcraft operating under the guise of ministry.

Jesus warned us: *"Every kingdom divided against itself is brought to desolation"* (Matthew 12:25). A Church that attacks itself cannot stand. We have created a culture where spiritual leaders are jealous of others rising. Instead of equipping, they tear down. Instead of blessing, they curse. If this is your heart, you need deliverance.

I have seen leaders go to the mountains to pray that another ministry will fail. I have seen pastors accuse others of witchcraft just to keep control. I have seen women silenced, abused, and oppressed by those who were meant to cover and protect them. What has happened to us?

Jesus said, *"The works that I do shall you do also"* (John 14:12). His ministry was not about suppression. It was about multiplication. He breathed on His disciples and released them to do greater works. But today, many leaders hold back others, afraid that someone else might shine brighter. If you are afraid of others rising around you, then you are not walking in the Spirit of Christ. The Spirit gives gifts to all. The Apostle Paul said, *"There are diversities of gifts, but the same Spirit"* (1 Corinthians 12:4).

True healing in the Church begins when leaders repent, when they step down from pedestals and return to the feet of Jesus, when they stop measuring success by offerings and start measuring it by obedience, love, and fruit.

You cannot claim to serve God and live in

hatred. You cannot lead others while rejecting the very heart of the Gospel. Jesus washed His disciples' feet. He restored Peter after his denial. He rebuked with love, not with shame. This is our example.

Many of today's ministries will never grow beyond their current state because the foundation is faulty. "*If the foundations are destroyed, what can the righteous do?*" (Psalm 11:3).

Healing comes through humility. It comes through truth. It comes when we, as the Body of Christ, admit we have failed to walk in love. You cannot heal a fly if your heart is full of hatred. You cannot cast out demons while partnering with pride. You cannot build a lasting ministry on control. These things may work for a time, but eventually, they crumble.

God is calling His Church back to love, back to purity, back to truth. Those who have built ministries on manipulation must repent. Those who have hurt others through spiritual control must seek forgiveness. Those who have turned from the example of Christ must return to Him.

The Church needs cleansing. The Church needs deliverance. The Church needs healing. Let every pastor, prophet, teacher, and leader examine their heart. If you have used your position to harm, now is the time to make it right. If you have silenced others out of fear or insecurity, repent. God is not impressed by numbers. He is not impressed by titles. He is looking for hearts that reflect His own. The love of God must return to the leadership of the Church. Without it, revival will never come. Let the Church be healed, one heart at a time.

Reflect and Respond

What other scriptures come to your mind about love in the church?

In what ways might your leadership or service need to be realigned with the servant-hearted example of Christ?

What step can you take today—whether repentance, restoration, or releasing others—to participate in healing the Body of Christ?

Chapter 9

A Returning to the Love of God

Revival does not begin in the pulpit. It begins in the heart. Not in the sound of our worship or the size of our buildings, but in the personal decision to love God again with everything we have. The Church today is crying out for revival, but many are looking for fire without first returning to love. True revival is not born in noise or numbers. It is born in surrender, in brokenness, and in the simple, profound affection for the One who first loved us.

The love of God is the path to revival. When we return to Him with pure hearts, He responds with healing and power. The prophet Hosea declared, *"Come, and let us return to the Lord; for He has torn, but He will heal us; He has stricken, but He will bind us up"* (Hosea 6:1). There is no healing without return. There is no outpouring without repentance. We must acknowledge how far we have drifted from the heart of God.

In our modern age, churches are often full of activity but lacking affection. Events continue, programmes increase, and strategies multiply, yet something eternal is missing. Our calendars are full, but our altars are empty. Many leaders are tired, burnt out, or chasing platforms, but God is not calling us to strive. He is calling us to abide. As Jesus said, *"Abide in Me, and I in you. As the branch cannot bear fruit of itself, unless it abides in the vine, neither can you, unless you abide in Me"* (John 15:4).

When Jesus asked Peter three times, "*Do you love Me?*" (John 21:15–17), He was not questioning Peter's leadership skills. He was probing his heart. Before Peter could feed the sheep, he had to be restored to love. That same question echoes through every generation. Revival begins when we can answer it with truth and tears. Not with performance, but with passion. Not with ability, but with affection.

The early Church turned the world upside down, not because they had the best resources or political influence, but because they were full of love. They were united in spirit and sacrificial in heart. "*Now the multitude of those who believed were of one heart and one soul... and great grace was upon them all*" (Acts 4:32–33). Unity is the fragrance of love. Grace is the atmosphere of revival.

We cannot have revival while harbouring

hatred. We cannot experience miracles while manipulating people. We cannot expect heaven to move while we tear each other down in prayer and in speech. Bitterness will always block the flow of the Spirit. Unforgiveness will always quench the fire of revival.

Returning to the love of God means real repentance. It means asking hard questions: Is this message birthed in love? Is this ministry structured around love? Is this leadership led by love? Paul exhorted the Corinthian Church, "*Let all that you do be done with love*" (1 Corinthians 16:14). That includes the unseen service, the way we speak to our families, the manner in which we correct others, and the posture with which we carry our calling.

The Church needs a personal revival before we can ever see a corporate one. We must each cry out, "Lord, revive me." Let the fire of God fall on our own hearts before we ask for it to fall on the stage. Let the Word of God wash every crooked motive. Let His love tenderise every hardened place.

God is not far. He is near. The delay is not on His part. The heavens are not closed. We are the ones who have wandered. We are the ones who have hardened our hearts. Revival is not waiting on heaven. Revival is waiting on humility. We must return. We must rebuild. We must remember the God who loved us even while we were yet sinners (Romans 5:8).

The greatest revival the world has ever seen will not bc lcd by thc most gifted. It will be led by the most surrendered. By those who have died to self and are alive in love. By those who do not use their platforms to promote themselves but to magnify Christ. By those who are more concerned with washing feet than gathering crowds.

Jesus said, "*By this all will know that you are My disciples, if you have love for one another*" (John 13:35). Revival is not just about signs and wonders. It is about love made visible. It is about a Church that walks like Christ, talks like Christ, and lives like Christ, not in formality, but in fullness.

Let us return to the Lord. Let us return to love. Let us repent of pride, bitterness, and unforgiveness. Let us rebuild the altars of prayer, purity, and unity. Let us become lovers of God once more, not merely ministers, leaders, or worshippers in name. When we do, healing will come. Deliverance will come. Power will come. Not because we shouted louder, but because we loved deeper. The path to revival is not paved with methods and strategies. It is paved with mercy. It is not driven by performance. It is led by love. Let the Church return. Let us return to love.

Reflect and Respond

Have I drifted into activity without affection—doing ministry without truly loving the One who called me?

In what areas of my life do I need to repent and return to my first love for God?

Is love the foundation of everything I do—in prayer, leadership, speech, and service?

CHAPTER 10

The Fear of the Lord

Revival cannot come without the fear of the Lord. The Church cannot be healed without reverence. Power cannot be sustained without righteousness. The Bible says, *"The fear of the Lord is the beginning of wisdom, and the knowledge of the Holy One is understanding"* (Proverbs 9:10). Without this foundation, we build our ministries on sand.

Jesus said, *"I am the true vine, and My Father is the vinedresser"* (John 15:1). He went on to say, *"Abide in Me, and I in you. As the branch cannot bear fruit of itself, unless it abides in the vine, neither can you, unless you abide in Me"* (John 15:4). To abide in Christ is to walk in love, in truth, and in the fear of God. Without Him, we can do nothing.

The fear of the Lord brings fruitfulness. It is not fear of punishment, but a holy reverence that keeps our hearts aligned with God. It checks our motives, convicts us of sin, and leads us into repentance. When we fear God, we cannot treat people any way we like. We cannot oppress, manipulate, or harm others without being grieved in our spirit.

There is a sickness in the Church today. Leaders who preach one thing and live another. Pastors who hurt people and feel no remorse. Ministers who use the gifts of others but refuse to release or empower them. People are being wounded in churches and silenced under spiritual control. This must stop.

If you have the fear of the Lord in your heart,

even when you make a mistake, your conscience will trouble you. You will go before God and cry, "*Lord, take this from me. It is not of You. Deliver me.*" *And God, in His mercy, will deliver you.* "*If we confess our sins, He is faithful and just to forgive us our sins and to cleanse us from all unrighteousness*" (1 John 1:9).

The fear of God guards our behaviour. It teaches us to love others, not because they deserve it, but because they are created in His image. "*He who oppresses the poor reproaches his Maker, but he who honours Him has mercy on the needy*" (Proverbs 14:31).

Today, many are preaching but living in rebellion. There are leaders who have not spoken to family members in decades, yet they stand in pulpits declaring, "Jesus is Lord." God knows who you are. You know who you are. If there is animosity in your heart and no desire for reconciliation, the fear of the

Lord is absent.

I speak not to condemn, but to call to repentance. I have walked through some of these things myself. I have seen leaders who used others for their own gain. I have experienced the pain of being used but never released. That is why I wrote this book. Not to bring the Church down, but to call it higher.

If you fear God, you will not mock others. You will not deceive. You will not trample people for your own benefit. You will not take what does not belong to you. You will not lead people astray while seeking your own gain. Love flows from godly fear which is reverence. True fear of the Lord produces compassion, mercy, and holiness. It causes us to treat others with dignity. It humbles us before God and before men.

Some will say, "But people have hurt me." Yes,

we all have stories. But that is no excuse to stop loving. Love them from a distance if needed, but do not stop praying. Pray for their hearts to be touched. Pray for their freedom. Pray for your own healing, too.

Today, churches are tearing each other apart. Leaders are publicly accusing one another. What used to be private is now exposed through the media. This is not the fault of the media. It is the mercy of God, calling us to accountability. Twenty years ago, these things could be hidden. Today, God is shining light.

Let every pastor, every leader, every believer ask themselves, "Do I fear God? Do I love what God loves?" If the answer is no, then now is the time to return, not to religion, but to reverence.

Some leaders are flying in private jets while their members suffer. They build empires while their people are crushed. This is not the Gospel. Jesus came not to be served, but to serve. If you fear God, you will be content with what He has given you. You will be generous. You will be just. You will not take the glory for what God has done. "*I am the Lord, that is My name; and My glory I will not give to another*" (Isaiah 42:8).

Many no longer preach the fear of the Lord. They preach favour, promotion, and success. But what is success without reverence? What is increase without integrity?

God is calling us back. Back to the Word. Back to prayer. Back to holiness. Back to humility. Back to the fear of the Lord. Let the Church repent. Let the leaders fall on their faces. Let the members cry out for mercy. Because without the fear of God, there can be no revival. And without love, there can be no life.

"Let us hear the conclusion of the whole matter: Fear God and keep His commandments, for this is man's all" (Ecclesiastes 12:13). The time is now. Return to reverence. Return to righteousness. Return to the fear of the Lord.

A Word on Prayer and the Love of God

Our prayer life must be completely submitted to the Holy Spirit if we are to see true revival in the Church. Prayer that is driven by routine, confined within our denomination, or motivated by self-interest will never usher in the kind of move that transforms hearts and nations. If the love of God is truly in our hearts, then our prayers must go beyond our local Church, our personal group, or our circle of influence.

Jesus said, *"Go into all the world and preach the gospel to every creature"* (Mark 16:15). This call is not limited to our ministry or our gathering. It is global. And if we are called to reach the world, then we must also learn to intercede for the Body of Christ across the world, not just for our own needs or our familiar group.

There are times when the Lord has laid names on my heart—people I did not know. I would receive just a name or a prompting, and I would pray. At first, I wanted to know who they were. I wanted to understand. But over time, I grew to realise that it was not about satisfying my curiosity. It was about obedience. It was about being led by the Spirit. The more we grow in the love of God, the more we are willing to pray without needing explanation. *"Likewise the Spirit also helps in our weaknesses. For we do not know what we should pray for as we ought, but the Spirit Himself makes intercession for us"* (Romans 8:26).

This is what it means to walk in the Spirit. You do not need a platform or a microphone to be effective. You just need a surrendered heart and a willingness to obey. When we allow the Holy Spirit to lead our prayers, He will stretch us beyond our four walls. He will cause us to pray for those we have never met. That is the love of God in action.

If we are only praying for our own Church to grow or for our denomination to flourish while ignoring the needs of others in the Body, then we are limiting God. Worse still, if we find ourselves praying against others out of envy, comparison, or pride, then we are not walking in love. We are becoming instruments of division rather than vessels of healing.

Galatians 6:2 says, *"Bear one another's burdens, and so fulfil the law of Christ"*. That is the law of love. We are called to pray for one another, not compete with one another. We are called to lift up, not tear down. When we are motivated by love, we cannot ignore the struggles of others. Even if another ministry is struggling, we pray. Even if a pastor has fallen, we pray. Even if the Church down the road is growing faster than ours, we still pray. Why? Because it is not about us. It is about the Kingdom of God.

We cannot expect revival while we are fighting one another in prayer. We must stop the silent warfare within the Church. Instead of praying against others, let us pray for them. Instead of hoping for their downfall, let us intercede for their restoration. This is how we prepare for a true move of God. *"If one member suffers, all the members suffer with it; or if one member is honoured, all the members rejoice with it"* (1 Corinthians 12:26).

The Lord is calling His Church back to love.

And that includes love in prayer. Not just love in speech or behaviour, but love in intercession. It is time to pray beyond our Church. Time to love beyond our circle. Time to partner with the Holy Spirit and pray the prayers that touch heaven and transform earth.

May the Lord help us. May He fill our hearts with divine love. And may our prayers reflect the breadth, length, depth, and height of His love for His Church and for the world. Amen.

Reflect and Respond

Do I truly walk in the fear of the Lord, or have I grown casual in how I treat others and handle spiritual responsibility?

Are my motives in ministry and prayer rooted in love, humility, and reverence—or are they driven by pride, comparison, or control?

In what ways is the Holy Spirit prompting me to return to purity, obedience, and the fear of the Lord?

CHAPTER 11

Let Love Lead

Revival does not begin with a crowd. It begins with a heart. Not a heart full of noise, pride, or activity, but a heart fully surrendered to the love of God. The Spirit of the Lord is calling His Church back to the place where it all began—back to love.

We have fasted, we have prayed, we have hosted events, but the question remains: have we returned to our first love? Jesus said in Revelation 2:4–5, *"Nevertheless I have this against you, that you have left your first love. Remember therefore from where you have fallen; repent and do the first works."*

Revival is not about stirring people's emotions. It is about awakening hearts. It is about restoring broken altars. It is about love—real love—for God, for people, and for His Word. If we miss that, we have missed everything.

Jesus prayed for the Church before He went to the cross. In John 17, He did not pray for bigger crowds or grander buildings. He prayed that we would be one. He prayed that the love which the Father had for Him would be in us. "*And I have declared to them Your name, and will declare it, that the love with which You loved Me may be in them, and I in them*" (John 17:26).

This is the love that births revival. This is the love that breaks chains. This is the love that heals churches. Yet, sadly, we have replaced it with rivalry. Pastors rising against pastors. Churches speaking against churches. Believers tearing each other down in prayer instead of lifting each other up.

If you go to the mountain to pray against another ministry, you are not working for God. You are working against Him. How can you pray down the very person Christ died for? When you hate your brother and still stand to preach, you are not carrying God's Spirit. You are walking in the flesh.

I have seen what happens when we pray against others. Ministries dry up. Hearts grow cold. People begin to follow personalities instead of Christ. But I have also seen what happens when love is restored, when leaders pray for other leaders, when churches bless other churches. When the body of Christ comes together, not to compete, but to complete each other, that is when revival breaks out.

There is a cry rising from the heart of the

Father—a cry for unity in His Church. He is calling us to stop tearing one another down and begin lifting each other up. If another church is growing, bless them. If another pastor is being used, pray for them. You are not their competitor. You are their co-labourer in the vineyard.

This rivalry among ministers must end. Too many have gone to the mountain not to seek God's will but to pray against their brother. What kind of gospel is this? How can we say we are following Christ and yet spend our time fighting those He has called?

We must return to a place of honour. A place where the success of another does not threaten us, but inspires us. A place where we cry together, rise together, and advance together. If we keep dividing ourselves, how will the world see the light? Jesus said, *"By this all will know that you are My disciples, if you have love for one another*" (John 13:35).

Let every pulpit resound with a call to love. Let every Church become a house of healing, not a battleground of pride. Let the Church in our day be known not for its scandals or its splits, but for its unity, humility, and love. Only then will we see the revival we have been crying out for.

God is calling us to return. He is calling us to put down our weapons and pick up His Word. He is calling us to stop defending our denominations and start demonstrating His love. True revival is not a move of man. It is a move of God. And God only moves where there is love.

We are not waiting on God. God is waiting on us. The Holy Spirit is ready to move, but He will not dwell where bitterness reigns. He will not flow through hearts filled with envy and pride. If we want revival, we must prepare the ground.

And that ground is love. Love that is patient. Love that is kind. Love that does not envy. Love that does not boast. Love that keeps no record of wrongs. Love that rejoices in the truth. This is the love described in 1 Corinthians 13. And this is the love that must return to the Church.

Do not wait for your church leader to change. Start with yourself. Return to prayer. Return to the Word. Return to obedience. Return to the love of God. Let your heart be the altar. Let your life be the offering.

This is not about performance. It is about presence. Not about how many songs we sing, but how much we are surrendered. God is not impressed by how loud we are. He is moved by how low we go. Revival flows through humility and love.

We are the generation that must get it right. Those who came before us laboured, and many have gone. Now it is our turn. Let us not waste it chasing titles, followers, or fame. Let us pursue love.

Jesus is coming back for a Church without spot or wrinkle. That Church will not be defined by its programmes, its platforms, or its polish. It will be defined by love. Let us return.

Father, ignite our hearts again. Return us to our first love. Let the fire of revival be lit once more, not on stages, but in secret places. Heal Your Church. Unite Your Body. And let love lead us. In Jesus' name. Amen.

A Prayer for Revival

Heavenly Father, we come before You with humble hearts, longing for a fresh outpouring of Your Spirit in our generation. Let the fire of Your love ignite our churches, our homes, and our hearts once again. Awaken within us a deep hunger for holiness, truth, and compassion. Let every cold heart be warmed by Your presence, and every weary soul be refreshed by Your power.

Revive us, O Lord, not for our name or glory, but so that Your Kingdom may come and Your will be done on earth as it is in heaven. Heal our land, restore our unity, and let Your love flow through us like a river that never runs dry.

May the Church rise in purity, in power, and in love. May the lost be found, the broken be mended, and the weary be renewed. Breathe on us again, Lord, and let revival begin in our hearts. In Jesus' name we pray. Amen.

Reflect and Respond

What is the Holy Spirit prompting you to change after reading this book—within your heart, your relationships, or your ministry?

How can you intentionally walk in love and unity moving forward, especially when it costs you comfort, recognition, or control?

Are you ready to be a vessel of revival in this generation? What steps will you take today to let love lead?

If this book blessed you, challenged you, or stirred something in your heart, I would be deeply grateful if you took a moment to leave a review on Amazon.

Your words matter–not just to me, but to those who are searching for truth, healing, and the love of God.

A simple sentence or two can help someone else discover this message and be transformed by His love. Thank you for reading and sharing this journey with me.

Comfort Ekundayo

Printed in Dunstable, United Kingdom

66548312R00068